ANDREW FULLER

WORK SMARTER, NOT HARDER

STUDY SKILLS FOR STUDENTS
WHO DON'T LIKE HOMEWORK

Published in 2024 by Amba Press, Melbourne, Australia
www.ambapress.com.au

© Andrew Fuller 2024

All rights reserved. No part of this book may be reproduced or transmitted in any form or by any means, electronic or mechanical, including photocopying, recording or by any information storage and retrieval system, without prior permission in writing from the publisher.

Cover design: Tess McCabe
Internal design: Amba Press
Editor: Rica Dearman

ISBN: 9781923215207 (pbk)
ISBN: 9781923215214 (ebk)

A catalogue record for this book is available from the National Library of Australia.

CONTENTS

Introduction		1
Chapter 1	Goal setting	5
Chapter 2	Completing homework quickly	17
Chapter 3	Memory tricks	25
Chapter 4	Writing essays and papers	35
Chapter 5	Making notes in class	41
Chapter 6	Exams	53
Chapter 7	It's never too late	61
More reading		65
About the author		66

INTRODUCTION

The book will help you do as well as you possibly can at school with the minimum amount of effort. It has been trialled and researched with thousands of students. It worked for them and as long as you apply these ideas, it will work for you.

We all know that school is about learning – both in the classroom and also at home, the latter in the form of homework. I can hear your groans about this last word from here…

But don't worry – I can help you.

It's true that I won't be able to help you get out of actually doing your homework, but I can help you to obtain the maximum effect in the minimum amount of time. Together, we can free up hours of your time where you would have otherwise been lying on the couch feeling exhausted, daydreaming and possibly just whingeing.

I can also help you get better marks in essays, work requirements and exams. To find out how we can do this, you've got to read on…

THE FUTURE BELONGS TO THOSE WHO **PLAN FOR IT.**

Colin Hayes (Australian horse trainer)

Introduction

True or false?

First, answer these questions about your attitude and habits regarding schoolwork and doing homework by circling either 'True' or 'False'.

I generally don't study for teachers I don't like	True	False
I usually wait until I'm too tired to do anything else before I start doing homework	True	False
I find it hard to concentrate	True	False
I spend a long time doing homework	True	False
Homework helps me to daydream	True	False
It takes a long time to get ready to do homework	True	False
I have to be in the right mood to do homework	True	False
I usually take notes in class	True	False
I usually take notes in class and then never look at them again	True	False
My notes are so boring even I can't stand to look at them	True	False
I lose the notes I do take	True	False
I leave work requirements to the last moment	True	False

I usually just learn enough to pass the subject I'm studying	True	False
I panic before tests and examinations	True	False
I 'freeze up' in exams and go blank	True	False

If you answered 'true' to any of these questions, this book can help you. Let's start at the beginning…

Why study or do homework?

If you are going to study or do homework, you'll need to have some sort of goal in mind. Whether it is to become the greatest rock legend, an actor, to have a fabulous apartment and be surrounded by adoring friends and fans, or simply just to survive Year 12 (or 8, 9, 10 or 11) so you never have to do it again, it is important to figure out your reason for doing homework.

The difference between people who achieve what they want in life and those who don't doesn't have much to do with how hard they work – it is the *way* they work that it is important. They decide on some goals and then work just hard enough to get there – no more, and no less.

Go to www.mylearningstrengths.com and complete an analysis of your learning strengths.

This will help you to learn how you are smart.

CHAPTER 1
GOAL SETTING

> A DREAM BECOMES A GOAL WHEN **ACTION IS TAKEN** TOWARD ITS ACHIEVEMENT.

Bo Bennett (American entrepreneur)

Setting goals can help you understand where you want to be in the future – whether this means in a year's time, five years' time or even further down the track. Once you have set yourself some goals, it can be easier for you to work out what you need to do in order to achieve them, to reach your desired future life.

When preparing a plan of action of how you can achieve your goals, consider both short- and long-term planning.

Short-term planning

The best way to plan to succeed is to decide what marks you want to get at school in advance. This helps you avoid putting in a lot of unnecessary work for marks you don't need. Remember, you only have to get the marks you need to do the job that you want.

Some schools simply mark 'Satisfactory' or 'Not satisfactory'; others go for As, Bs, Cs, Ds, Es and Fs. It doesn't matter which system your school uses; it is still useful to plan your marks in advance.

One way of doing this is to decide in advance what marks you want to get for particular subjects – the subjects that will help you achieve your future goals. This way, you won't end up doing endless hours of homework to get good marks in subjects that won't help you achieve your future goals. You can then put more effort into the homework and study that will go toward achieving higher marks for your chosen career path and future life.

Planning the marks you want to get takes a bit of time, but as you will see, it's time well spent.

Here is a formula that can help you work out how to do this:

1. First, write down the names of all the subjects you are doing this year.
2. Then, write down the mark that you are prepared to work toward getting in each subject.
3. Next, write down the number of hours of homework you are prepared to put in each week to get those marks.
4. Add up all of the hours of homework.
5. Ask yourself: "Am I really prepared to spend all of that time doing homework?"
    a. If the answer is "no", go back to your desired marks list and consider whether you should lower the marks you want to get.
    b. If the answer is "yes", then it's time to work out the best way of doing homework so that it has the least negative effect on your life.

Have a look at the following example from a Year 12 student.

Goal setting

Subject	Desired mark	Homework hours per week
English	B	3
Maths methods	C	3
Information Technology	B	2
Psychology	A	3
SOS	D	2
Revolutions	C	3
Total		**16 hours**

Using this example, you could work out your study time in any of the following ways that suits you best:

- 16 hours divided by 6 days a week (so that you have 1 day off) = 2½ hours of study per day, 6 days a week

    Or

- 2 hours of study on 4 days during the week (Monday to Thursday), plus 8 hours over the weekend

    Or

- 3¼ hours of study over 5 days

Or

- 4 hours of study on any 4 evenings

Or

- 8 hours of study on any 2 evenings

Have a go at working out your own study time according to the formula described above. Fill in the table below.

Subject	Desired mark	Homework hours per week
Total		

Goal setting

Now, calculate how long you are prepared to spend studying and on what days:

_____

_____

_____

_____

_____

_____

_____

Sure, there will be people who will tell you that doing homework slowly and regularly is the best way, but everybody works differently. We all have particular times of the day when we zombie out, and at other times we are our usual brilliant selves. We just need to find the time of day and method that works best for each of us. After all, we're not all robots.

It's just as important to set aside some time for non-study pursuits. Think about the activities that are important to you: sports, hanging out with friends, watching TV, going to the movies, music practice, etc., and make sure you set that time aside in a weekly planner. Then work out your study time in the best way to achieve the marks you want to get.

Long-term planning

Imagine that you have just received a postcard from yourself in the future, say, five or so years from now. Take a moment to answer the following questions.

Where would you like it to come from?

_____

_____

_____

_____

What would you like it to say?

_____

_____

_____

_____

What sort of person would you like to have sent it?

_____

_____

_____

_____

Goal setting

What would make them happy?

_____

_____

_____

Now imagine that a current news programme is interviewing you about your successes in six years' time. What would you tell the interviewer? What could you do now to get to the place you want to be in six years' time?

Subject	Desired mark	Estimated amount of homework hours per week	Actual amount of time spent on homework
Total			

THERE IS NO SUCH THING AS A **FAVOURABLE WIND** TO SOMEONE WHO DOES NOT KNOW WHERE THEY ARE GOING.

adapted from Seneca (Roman philosopher)

Goal setting

Once you've worked out the amount of homework that you are prepared to do, try to set aside a regular time to do it each weekday. Most people find that if they have to do homework, it is better to do it at the same time every day and in the same place. They also find that brief bursts of homework are better than spending long hours at it.

CHAPTER 2
COMPLETING HOMEWORK QUICKLY

> WHETHER YOU THINK YOU CAN OR YOU CAN'T, YOU ARE **PROBABLY RIGHT.**

Henry Ford (American entrepreneur)

We would all love to get our homework over and done with as quickly as possible – but you also want to put in the right amount of effort to get the best results.

30-minute study experiment

Have a go at the following experiment…

For one week, set aside a 30-minute time slot each day to do your homework. For example, this could be from 4pm till 4.30pm, or the half hour before you have dinner. Ask your family to help you by reducing the distractions around the house during your chosen half hour. During this time, it's a good idea for anything you are not directly working on, to be switched off or in another room so that it won't distract you.

Set yourself up in a quiet location where you can concentrate, be that at a desk in your bedroom, in a parent's study or at the kitchen table. Make sure you have all the things you need to do your homework: books, pens, rulers, calculators, laptop, etc. To prepare yourself for making the most of your homework time, make an entry in your diary for the major aim of each subject every week.

Then, tell your family when your half hour of homework is starting so that they can leave you alone to do it. If you like, you can ask them to come in and tell you when it's time to stop.

For half an hour, work as fast and as hard as you can. Try to get as much homework done as possible during this time.

At the end of the allocated half hour, whether you've timed it yourself or your family has come to tell you the time is up, you can stop.

That should be the end of work for that day.

Anything that is not completed in the half hour should be added to a to-do list and done the next day at the same time, in the same place.

Are you ready to try this out? What have you got to lose? Go on and have a go at it!

After one week, see how you've gone and ask yourself:

- Have you started getting more homework completed in a short time? If not, keep with the 30 minutes a day until you feel you've become more effective.

- Do you feel you've managed 30 minutes fairly easily? If so, it's now time to work out how much homework time you *should* be setting aside each weekday, to get the marks at school that you want to get.

Some people will stick with 30 minutes (and add a little bit of memory time, say, 10 minutes a day – more on that later), while others in more senior years have one, two or even more 30-minute periods.

Example homework schedules

Let's look at some students and their homework schedules. The following table shows how two students plan their 30 minutes of homework every day around other activities:

Time	Harry	Hermione
3.30pm	School finishes	School finishes
4pm	Arrive home and eat	Sports practice
4.30pm	Homework	Sports practice
5pm	See friends	Arrive home and eat
5.30pm	TV	TV
6pm	Memory time (10 minutes), then more TV	Homework
6.30pm	Dinnertime	Dinnertime
7pm	Relaxation	Memory time, then relaxation

Have a go at filling in the below table to see how you could develop your own homework pattern:

Time	Your pattern
3.30pm	
4pm	
4.30pm	
5pm	
5.30pm	
6pm	
6.30pm	
7pm	

Memory time

There is one important thing to remember: memory time is *not* homework time.

Homework time is the time that you set aside to complete work requirements, such as writing essays and finishing worksheets. It's the sort of stuff that keeps you up with your class and keeps you out of trouble.

> IF YOU HAVE GOOD HABITS, TIME BECOMES YOUR ALLY. ALL YOU NEED IS **PATIENCE.**

James Clear (American writer)

The problem is that once you've done it, homework is not very easy to remember. And in tests and exams, schools often expect you to remember the work that you've done. For that reason, I suggest you set aside some separate time called 'memory time' to help you recall what you've learned. This is a portion of time that you set aside once a day – or even once a week – to put together all of the things that you've learned.

What helps memory is not just reading over your notes, but also organising or changing them in a way that makes sense to you or is memorable to you.

Memory reviews of homework should occur regularly, with the first block of time being for 10 minutes, one hour after you have finished your homework, and then five minutes the following day. Once this becomes a habit, you will probably find that spending just two minutes a week remembering and organising each segment of work will be enough.

CHAPTER 3
MEMORY TRICKS

THE BEST PREPARATION FOR TOMORROW IS DOING **YOUR BEST TODAY**.

H Jackson Brown Jr (American author)

Learning and remembering stuff can be hard. And the more boring your work is, the harder it is to remember it – so make it interesting!

Information is most easily remembered when you don't just learn it, but when you use it in some way.

Use acronyms to aid you

Acronyms are words where each letter stands for something else. Some examples include:

DIY – **D**o **I**t **Y**ourself

LOL – **L**augh **O**ut **L**oud

NASA – **N**ational **A**eronautics and **S**pace **A**dministration

You get my drift…

When it comes to schoolwork and remembering what you've learned, you can create your own acronyms to help you remember what you learned.

For each subject or area of study, build a series of keywords that will become 'acronyms' that you will try to put information into.

For example, one way of remembering Isaac Newton's discovery of gravity when an apple fell on his head could be to use the acronym **NIRVANA**, as below:

Newton's
Ideas
Relativity
Vague
Awaiting
Nonging (on his head with an)
Apple

Generally, it is better to use terms or phrases that will be really memorable to you. Some of the skills outlined in this book could be memorised using the following acronym:

Set your main priorities for each subject every week
Update notes and review them regularly
Construct acronyms to help you remember
Create achievable goals
Endeavour to achieve a goal each week
Study at times when you are alert
Set it up to be interesting and compelling

Another example of an acronym is contained in the following guidelines on how to fail:

Study when you are tired
Try to ignore instructions
Under-prepare

Frighten yourself – tell yourself you can't do it
Fool about a lot (and give up)
Upset yourself at key moments
Persistently plague your parents

Acronyms can also be sentences of words, for example:

Every **G**ood **B**oy **D**eserves **F**avour

This is one way of remembering the order of musical notes on the treble clef: E, G, B, D and F.

Another example is:

Never **E**at **S**hredded **W**heat

This is an easy way to remember the compass directions: North, East, South, West.

Now it's your turn. Have a go at putting together acronyms that will help you remember when you study. Try some out here:

Having made a series of acronyms, you can then build a 'super-acronym' that will lead you to all of the other acronyms you've set up.

Check out the following list of acronyms that can create a super-acronym:

Set priorities
Update notes
Construct acronyms
Create goals
Endeavour to achieve goals
Study at alert times
Set it up to be interesting

Newton's
Ideas
Relativity
Vague
Awaiting
Nonging
Apple

Interesting or
Dull
Ideas
Organised in a
Tickle

Develop
Exciting
Creative
Images (mental pictures)
Do a brief memory time
Every week

Every
Last student
Even
Pets of teachers want
Homework
And exams
Never to
Take over their life

Study when tired
Try to ignore instructions
Under-prepare
Frighten yourself
Fool about
Upset yourself
Plague your parents

These can then be summarised and memorised in the following super-acronym **SNIDES**:

Success
Nirvana
Idiot
Decide
Elephant
Study when tired

A journey to remembering

Another way of remembering a list of items, words or ideas is to think of a journey that you know really well – so well that you could almost do it with your eyes closed. It might be the way from your home to your school or from your bedroom to the kitchen. It doesn't matter, as long as the trip is well known to you. If there are 10 things you want to remember, pick 10 features along the trip and then remember one thing for each part of the trip.

TEACHERS ARE HUMAN!

Another way to work smarter, not harder, is to learn the lesson that teachers are human.

Believe it or not, but teachers *are* human, and they actually like to help students who express interest in the subjects they're teaching. If you fall behind or feel that you've slacked off for some time and want to make an effort to catch up, it is worth being honest with your teacher and asking them for advice about strategies. They really do want to help you do well in your subjects.

Librarians also often like to help and are particularly valuable in suggesting key words for research topics on the internet and through other library resources, so seek them out should you need some assistance.

TEACHERS CAN **OPEN THE DOOR**, BUT YOU MUST ENTER IT YOURSELF.

Chinese proverb

CHAPTER 4
WRITING ESSAYS AND PAPERS

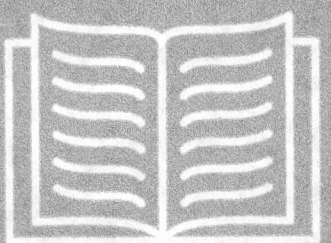

> YOU DON'T HAVE TO BE GREAT TO START, BUT YOU HAVE TO **START TO BE GREAT**.

Zig Ziglar (American author)

If you are going to work smarter, not harder, you might as well enjoy the schoolwork you have to do. If you get asked to write an essay or paper, try to tie it into an area of your personal interests, such as football, netball, music or movies. It doesn't really matter which, just try to find an angle that you are interested in and use it to build your motivation.

The following points may help you in developing a great essay (note the super-acronym to help you remember these points):

1. **C**hoose an interesting topic.
2. **R**esearch your topic online or at the library.
3. **E**stablish an argument around a central idea.
4. **A**dd a broad, brief outline in three lines:

    This essay or paper argues _____

    because _____

    and finds _____ .

6. **T**ake your research further and put each idea that you have on a card.
7. **E**stablish an outline after shuffling the cards.
8. **G**et started on writing the outline and a first draft.

9. Research some more should you need to.
10. Expand your essay into a second draft – remember, there is no such thing as good writing, there is only good rewriting.
11. Address the final tasks of conducting a spellcheck and proofread.
12. Test how it sounds by reading it aloud.
13. Edit it should it need it at this stage.
14. See if someone else will proofread it for you.
15. Set up some acronyms to remember key points.
16. Also establish super-acronyms to help you remember.
17. You've finished – enjoy some time off!

Have a go at writing an essay based on this super-acronym, or alternatively, create your own super-acronym to help you develop a great essay.

EDUCATION IS THE MOST POWERFUL WEAPON WHICH YOU CAN USE TO **CHANGE THE WORLD.**

Nelson Mandela

GIVING A TALK

If you have to give a talk to a class group, using the following acronym to remember the points below may help:

Find the three main things you want to say.

Really think about what would interest the audience and what they would be likely to remember.

Ensure that you develop the talk to finish with a particular sentence for optimal effect.

Avoid only reading from your notes if you can; use cards with keywords as prompts.

Keep to the allocated time – you will lose points if your talk falls too short, or too long.

Obtain a few extra speaking points by adding in some humour where you can.

Use aids such as overheads, posters, music, poems and films for extra effect and to gain additional points.

Try to practise in front of the mirror at home a few times in preparation.

CHAPTER 5
MAKING NOTES IN CLASS

> THE MORE YOU LEARN, THE MORE YOU REALISE HOW MUCH YOU **DON'T KNOW.**

Albert Einstein

Some people try to write down everything a teacher says in a class. They are working harder, but not smarter. Other people don't write very much at all, relying instead on their memories. These people are not working harder or smarter.

Effective note making requires you to pick out the main ideas in a class, or from a book or article, and to then link these to other ideas that seem important. Think: what are the three most important points of this lesson?

How to make memorable notes

One of the best ways to organise information is to create notes.

From 2001 onward, with teachers from around the world, I conducted 'practical intelligence projects' looking for some of the more powerful ways to help students learn. The note-making system outlined here evolved from those discussions.

Essentially, it is an adaptation of the Cornell method of note-making and involves you writing a heading for the topic at the top of the page and then dividing it into three sections:

1. In a small section like a sidebar, write the most important bits of information or the key ideas.
2. In a larger section, write your main notes.

3. At the bottom, convert the same knowledge into a visual; a Venn diagram is ideal, but a bubble or concept map can also work.

Here is an example of how your note-making can look:

Topic heading	
Write the key ideas here	Write your main notes here
Create a visual representation such as a Venn diagram here	

By using this note-making system, you have transformed the same bit of knowledge into three different formats and increased the retention of that knowledge.

The problem is that it takes human beings 24 repetitions of anything to get to 80 per cent of competence. How can I get you to repeat anything 24 times? Let me show you how to give your memory a hand.

Give your memory a hand

Once you have finished a topic at school, make a summary hand; this is a repetition method to help your memory. If you are unsure about when you are starting a new topic, ask your teacher to tell you.

Cut out a cardboard shape of your hand. Use different-coloured pieces of cardboard for different subjects.

On one side of the cardboard hand, write the five most important pieces of knowledge about a topic – one on each finger and thumb. Some examples might be:

- *Five phases of art history*: Renaissance, Neoclassicism, romanticism, modern, contemporary.
- *Five types of chemical reactions*: combustion, synthesis, decomposition, acid-based, single and double displacement.

In the palm area, either draw a Venn diagram or write a more detailed summary of the topic in point form.

Then, turn your summary hand over and write a question you can use to test your memory of the topic, such as, "What are the five main phases of art history?" or "What are five types of chemical reactions?"

Test yourself once a week. Shuffle all the hands you have created this year and with the question side toward you, see if you can answer them. Then, turn over the hand and see if you were correct.

Work Smarter, Not Harder

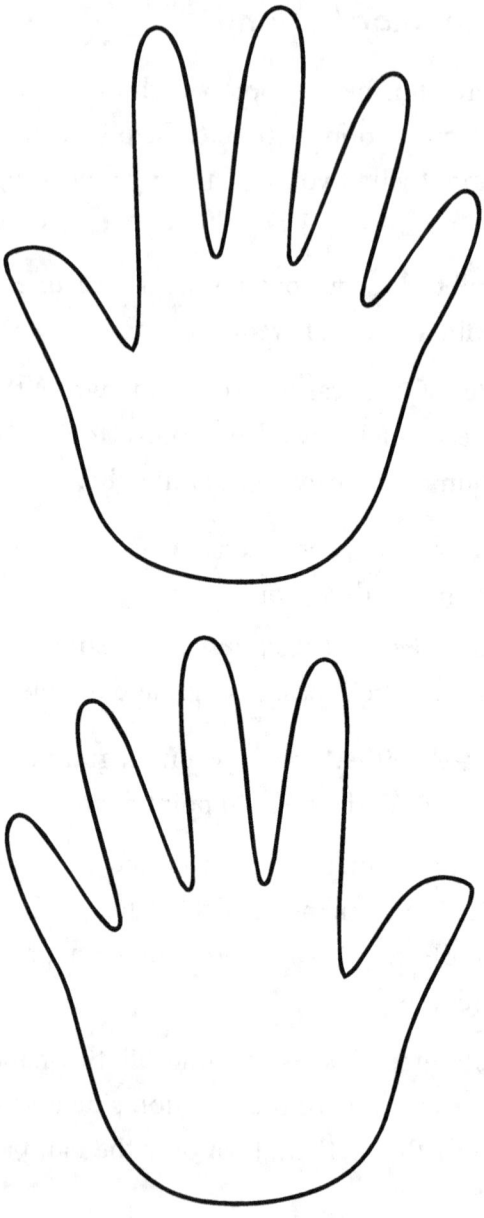

Put those you answered correctly into one pile and those you got wrong into another. Clearly, you may need to do some more work to understand the ones you didn't answer correctly.

The advantage of giving your memory a hand is that revision occurs throughout the year once a week, and this increases your memory and understanding.

Other ways to show main ideas is by underlining them or placing the main ideas in a margin to one side of a page. In reviewing an article or book, you may want to note the main ideas paragraph by paragraph, as per the following table.

	Main idea	Secondary ideas
Paragraph 1		
Paragraph 2		
Paragraph 3		
Paragraph 4		
Paragraph 5		

Experiment with different ways and choose the way that helps you to link ideas to one another.

Mind maps

Many people more easily remember pictures and diagrams rather than words. This is particularly true if you use vivid images, symbols and colours. For this reason, mind maps (as developed by Tony Buzan) can be incredibly effective for some people. Mind maps are visual, sometimes colourful, maps that use a central image or concept that is surrounded by different ideas, which are then linked to each other by lines or arrows.

Mind maps can also create links in your head about the connections between one idea and another. I've put together an example of a mind map on study skills and methods, to give you an idea of how these work. You would usually use different-coloured pens or pencils to indicate different areas of thought or to highlight areas of greater importance.

Making notes in class

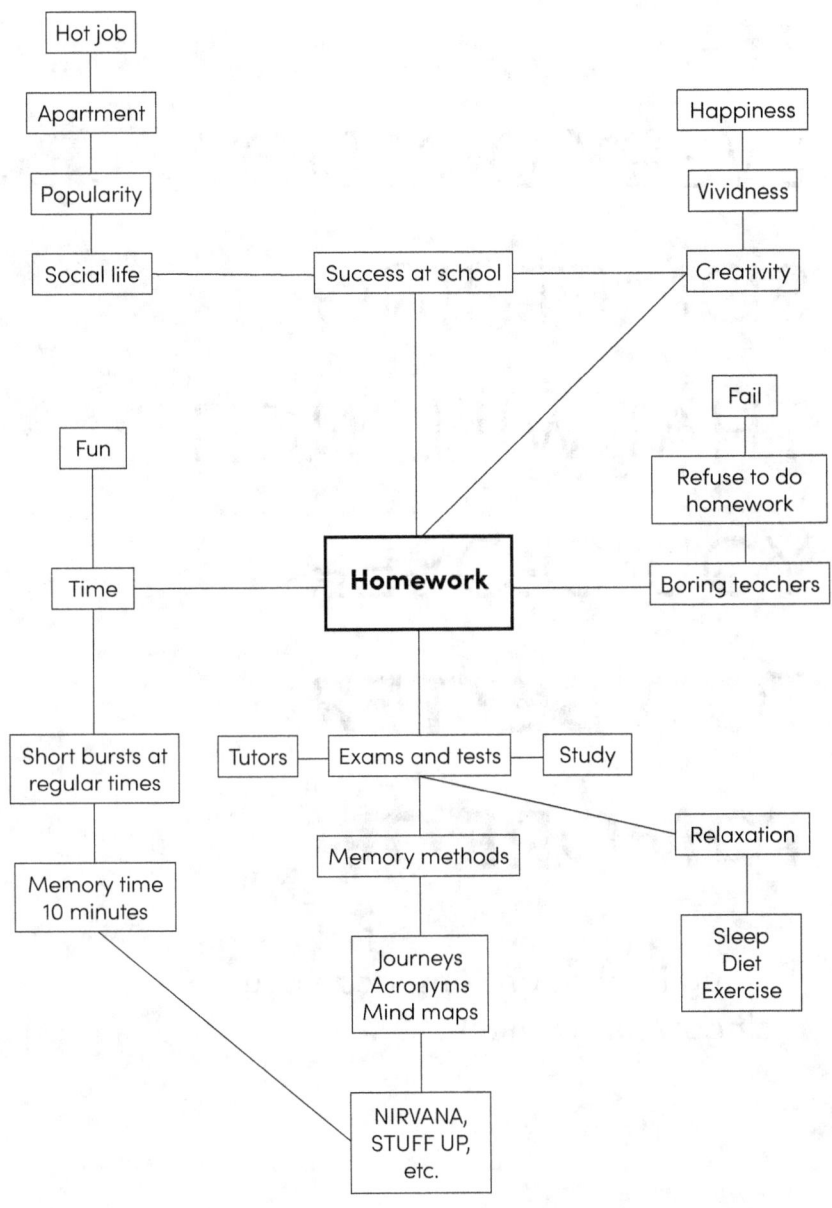

EVERY DAY DO SOMETHING THAT WILL INCH YOU CLOSER TO A **BETTER TOMORROW**.

Doug Firebaugh (American country singer/songwriter)

As you can see, the main idea is placed at the centre of the mind map, with different ideas creating pathways and linkages. This can be done for a particular class, a whole semester or even an entire year of work. I would suggest that mind maps are probably best used to try to summarise a semester's work in a particular subject and can be worked on once each week. You can use a different mind map for each of your subjects.

This approach is especially useful if you are an artistic person or someone who remembers pictures more easily than words. If you are going to use mind maps as a regular method of revising notes, it is probably worth buying Tony Buzan's book on the topic.

If you need to remember a mind map, make sure you review it regularly.

Have a go at producing a mind map on a topic of your choice. Try something unrelated to schoolwork as a practice, for example, it could be on a sport that you play, a movie or TV programme you enjoy or a hobby that you may have.

Use the structure on the next page to develop your mind map.

Work Smarter, Not Harder

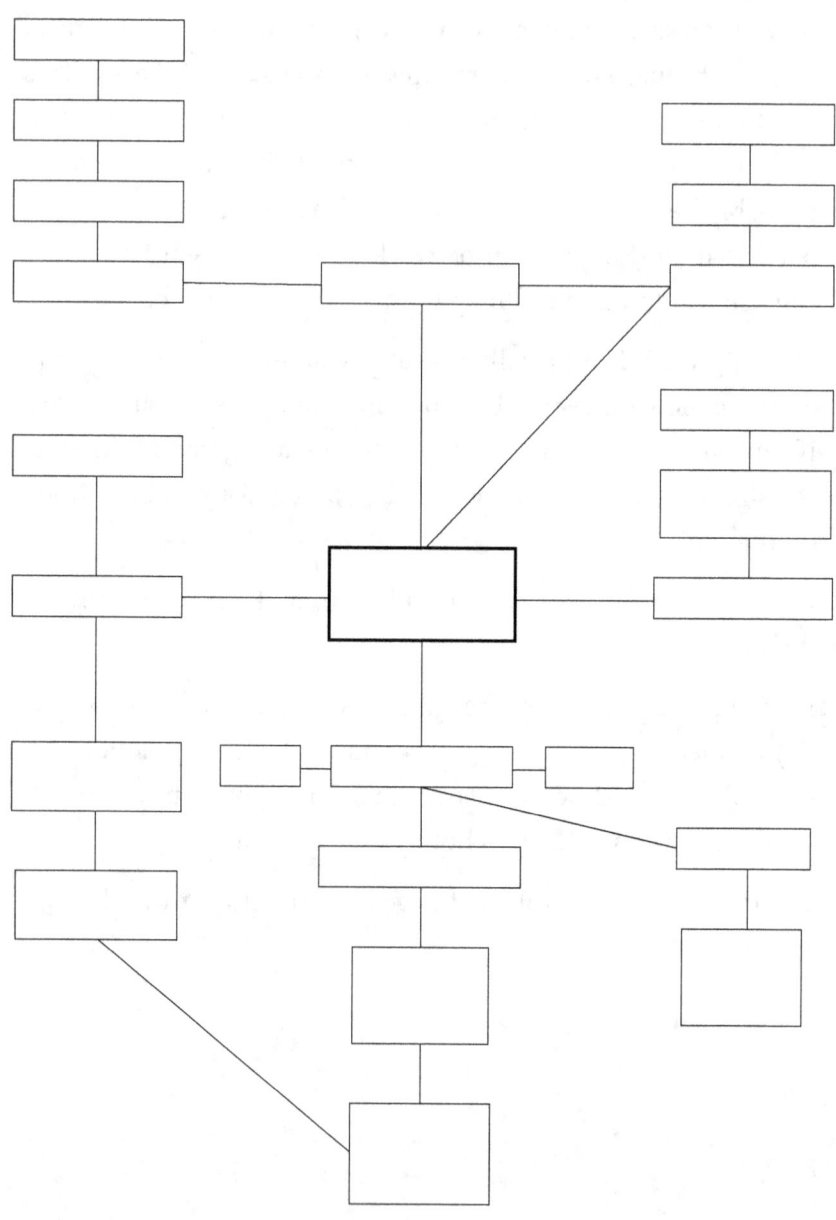

CHAPTER 6
EXAMS

> # THE MORE **YOU LEARN**, THE MORE **YOU EARN**.

Warren Buffett (American businessman)

There are many tricks to doing well in exams. Firstly, if at all possible, get your hands on examples of past exam papers. Look at the questions and try to break them down into smaller segments, then practise answering by developing skeleton answers. Skeleton answers may not be full answers, but these can be mini answers that summarise the main ideas you would want to convey in a full answer during an actual exam.

Discuss past exam questions with others and find out how they go about answering various questions. Remember, no one gets it right the first time; it is a matter of practising how to answer a question, practising some more, and then improving.

Just like sport, music, art, dance, driving a car, playing an instrument or almost any activity you can think of, people don't just do it once and then say either, "Well, that's as good as I can do" or, "I'm no good at this". Exams are the same. You just need to practise how to answer exam questions well.

The countdown to exams

Use the time leading up to your exams wisely. Here are some guides for how to work smarter, not harder, when studying.

12 to 9 days before an exam	• Review your written notes – skim read first for the main and secondary ideas. • If you haven't already done so, list the main and secondary ideas. • If you are writing on set texts, write mini essays on different angles of the book.
8 to 6 days before an exam	• Develop condensed notes and review your own notes. • Build acronyms, journeys, mind maps and any other associations that will help you to connect ideas and remember them.
7 to 4 days before an exam	• Work with others to develop strategies and possible responses for the exam. • Wherever possible, use past exam questions.
2 and 1 days before an exam	• Develop a power list or super-acronym. • Don't work too hard the night before – if you are really worried, spend the time sleeping and then wake up and go through your summary lists. • Focus on what you can do.

The morning of the exam

It is important that you are well rested so that you can go into the exam room feeling as comfortable as possible.

Eat breakfast – even if you feel nervous and not hungry, eat something as you'll need the energy to get you through to the end of the exam.

Review your notes, then transfer your condensed notes to another piece of paper without referring to your notes. This is a good way of practising what you have learnt.

In the exam room

On exam day, take a few deep breaths if you're feeling nervous, and know that you can only do the best that you can do.

Here are some tips to help you get through the exam as successfully as possible:

1. Fill in all of the administrative bits like your name and student number.
2. Skim read the instructions first, then read them again more thoroughly (don't be put off by other people picking up their pens).
3. Use the reading time constructively – read instructions, note sections and questions, read questions carefully and decide which ones you will do.

4. Keep a scrap piece of paper next to you to jot down notes, acronyms you have created and any other ideas as you write.

5. Plan your answers. As soon as you are instructed to start writing, immediately write down any quotes or formulae that you have memorised. While this takes time, it frees up your mind to focus on the task at hand, and you can then include these quotes or formulae when you need them.

6. Divide up the time sensibly; do multiple choice questions first, which can be quicker, then write essays using plans made earlier.

7. Complete the parts of the exam that you can do best, first.

8. Keep an eye on the time, and be careful not to spend too long on one section so that you have enough time to complete the rest of the exam.

9. If you get stuck, move on – don't sit there doing nothing, you can come back to it later. Highlight the question to help you to remember to come back to it later.

10. Breathe properly – every so often, give yourself a minute to gather your wits.

11. Don't leave early – even if you have finished everything, you'll be surprised at the ideas that will come to you when you take some time to relax.

> IF WE ALL DID THE THINGS WE ARE CAPABLE OF DOING, WE WOULD LITERALLY **ASTOUND OURSELVES.**
>
> Thomas Edison (inventor)

After the exam

When it's over, it's over. Don't spend time doing a post-exam analysis with your friends. There is no point worrying over how you might have gone, as it's too late to change anything now. You've got better things to do, so go and do them!

PHYSICAL HEALTH

It is difficult to do well at school if you are an overstressed couch potato who doesn't sleep or eat well. Try to take care of yourself by getting enough sleep and exercise, and eating a healthy, balanced diet. The point is to put homework into its place so that you can enjoy the other aspects of your life.

Remember, you don't need to succeed any better than the course or career that you want to get into requires. Not everyone needs to be a rocket scientist. So, if that's not your aim, then don't stress about it. Just try your best to get the marks that you want.

CHAPTER 7
IT'S NEVER TOO LATE

DON'T TELL ME HOW ROCKY THE SEA IS, JUST **BRING THE SHIP IN**.

Lou Holtz (former football coach)

So, it's late in the year, you've slacked off and now you find it's time for you to knuckle down and get serious.

The ideas in this book can be applied at any stage of the year, so it is never too late to begin working smarter, not harder. **If you feel like it's too late, it's not.**

Go through the goals that you have for each of your subjects. Review what pieces of work are overdue in each subject and complete the table on page 10 to work out how much time it will take.

Consider going to teachers and letting them know that you are going to make an effort to catch up, and ask for their advice. They will be only too happy to help.

Adults can tend to think that this is a good time to provide you with that moral lecture that starts off with, "Well, if you'd done your homework in the first place…" or, "If you'd listened to me when I said go and do your homework, you wouldn't be in this situation now". Try not to get too upset by this and don't waste your precious time arguing with them. They think they are doing their duty as parents or teachers and actually believe they are being helpful. (The poor, misguided souls!)

Contemplate asking your family to help you by assisting in a homework 'working bee' over one weekend. Of course, they don't have to do the homework, but they can help organise things, suggest ideas, read key textbooks and summarise ideas, bring you cool drinks, mop your feverish brow and generally look after you.

In extreme cases where it really seems like you can't possibly catch up, select three subjects that you want to pass in and just concentrate on the work due in those subjects.

MORE READING

If you would like to do more reading, check out the following sources:

- Buzan, T. (1995). *Use Your Head*, BBC Books.
- Francis, S. (2023). *Study Skills for Ambitious Senior Students: The High-Performance Advantage of the 8 Superhabits of Study.* Amba Press.
- Francis, S. (2024). *Exam Skills Handbook: How to Study and Perform Better in Exams.* Amba Press.
- Francis, S., & Nagel, M. C. (2023). *Your High-Performance Guide to Study and Learning: 20 Key Habits for Getting the Most Out of Your Study Time.* Amba Press.
- O'Brien, D. (2018). *How to Develop a Brilliant Memory Week by Week: 52 Proven Ways to Enhance Your Memory Skills.* ROH.

ABOUT THE AUTHOR

Andrew Fuller has recently been described as an "interesting mixture of Billy Connolly, Tim Winton and Frasier Crane", and as someone who "puts the heart back into psychology". As a clinical psychologist, Andrew works with many schools and communities in Australia and internationally, specialising in the wellbeing of young people and their families. He is an Honorary Fellow at the University of Melbourne.

www.ingramcontent.com/pod-product-compliance
Lightning Source LLC
Chambersburg PA
CBHW071127130526
44590CB00056B/2908